PLANT STRUCTURE AND CLASSIFICATION

JOSEPH MIDTHUN   SAMUEL HITI

BUILDING BLOCKS

SCIENCE

I0111448

WORLD BOOK

www.worldbook.com

World Book, Inc.
180 North LaSalle Street
Suite 900
Chicago, Illinois 60601
USA

For information about other World Book publications,
visit our website at www.worldbook.com
or call 1-800-WORLDBK (967-5325).
For information about sales to schools and libraries,
call 1-800-975-3250 (United States),
or 1-800-837-5365 (Canada).

Building Blocks of Science:
  Plant Structure and Classification
ISBN: 978-0-7166-7882-3 (trade, hc.)
ISBN: 978-0-7166-7890-8 (pbk.)
ISBN: 978-0-7166-2965-8 (e-book, EPUB3)

Acknowledgments:
Created by Samuel Hiti and Joseph Midthun
Art by Samuel Hiti
Text by Joseph Midthun
Special thanks to Syril McNally

TABLE OF CONTENTS

There is a glossary on page 30. Terms defined in the glossary are in type **that looks like this** on their first appearance.

All plants are **organisms**.

An organism is a living thing.

You're an organism too...

...but plants live in different ways.

Plants find a way to succeed in almost every corner of Earth.

They grow on mountaintops, in oceans, and also in deserts.

Plop

Some plants even grow in the snow!

Look around! You'll probably recognize a plant, or at least something that came from a plant.

Without plants, humans could not survive.

Most of the oxygen in the air you breathe comes from plants.

Almost all of the food you eat comes from plants or...

sniff sniff

...from animals that eat plants.

munch munch

Hey, cut that out!

5

STUDYING PLANTS

The study of plants is called **botany,** and scientists who study plants are known as **botanists.**

Plants are classified according to **common descent,** that is—

—by dividing them into groups that share a common ancestor.

Closely related plants share many similarities.

Botanists compare plants by their **traits,** including their overall appearance...

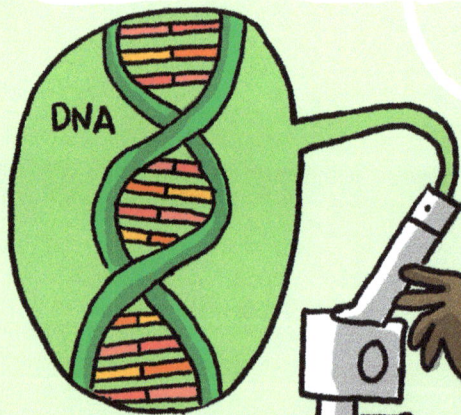

DNA

...their internal structure...

...and the form of their reproductive organs.

Just as all animals have certain **structures** or behaviors in common, plants have certain characteristics in common, too.

Like animals, plants come in all different shapes and sizes.

However, unlike animals, plants do not have to eat other things to get energy.

All plants have the ability to make their own food right inside the plant itself.

Some plants do trap and eat small insects, but only for nutrients—

—not energy.

7

SCIENTIFIC CLASSIFICATION

Taxonomy is the science of naming and classifying plants and other living things.

Scientific classification is a system of taxonomy used to organize all these different groups of organisms based on how closely they are related.

You are classified as a part of the animal kingdom.

These organisms are classified as a part of the **plant kingdom**.

There are several different levels of scientific classification between **domain** and **species**.

One of the largest groupings is called a **kingdom**.

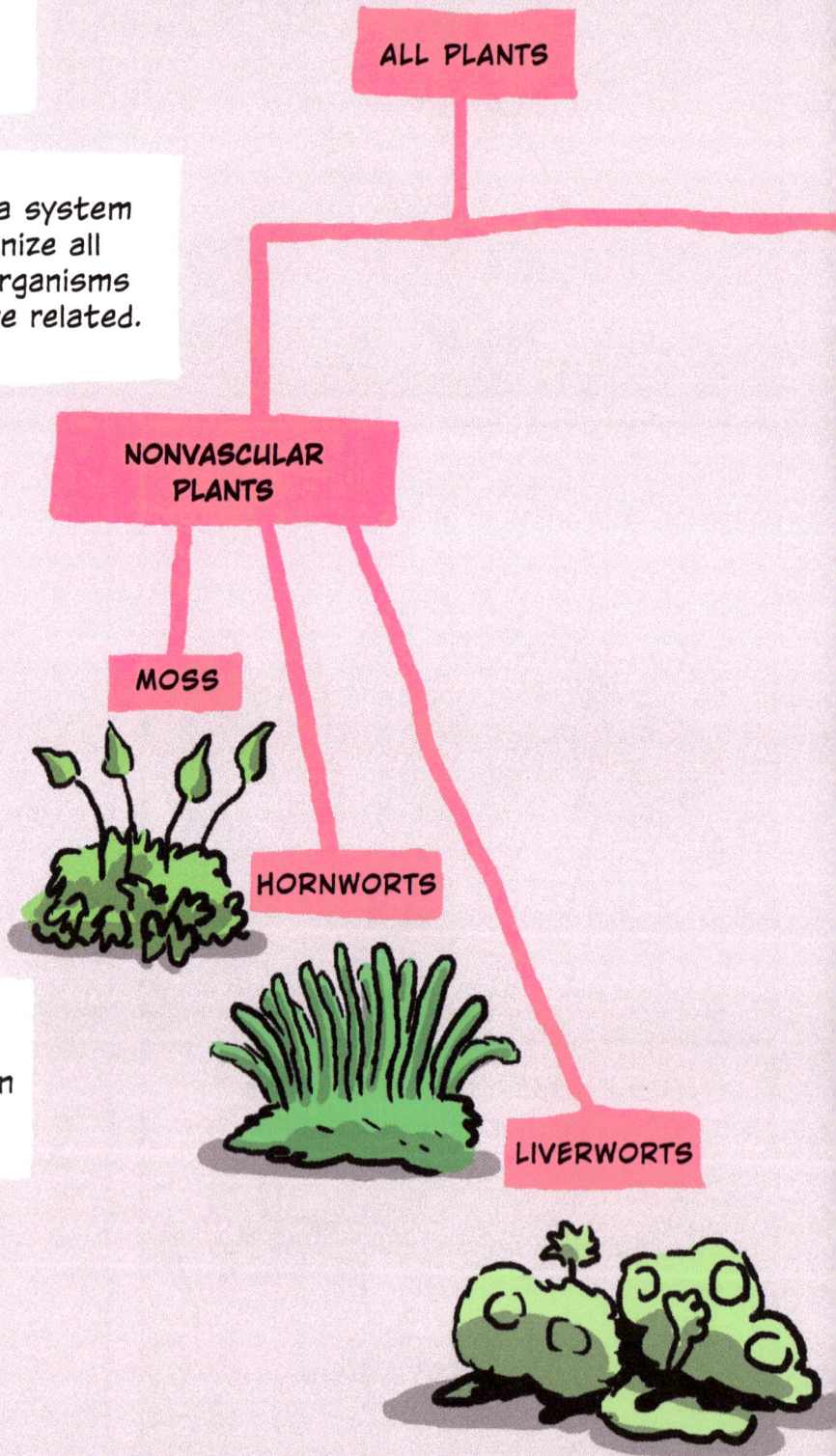

ALL PLANTS

NONVASCULAR PLANTS

MOSS

HORNWORTS

LIVERWORTS

Moving down through the levels, plants with more and more similarities are grouped together.

Plants that share the same **order**, **family**, and **genus**, are more closely related.

Whereas species that share the same order, **class**, or **division** may have a more distant relation.

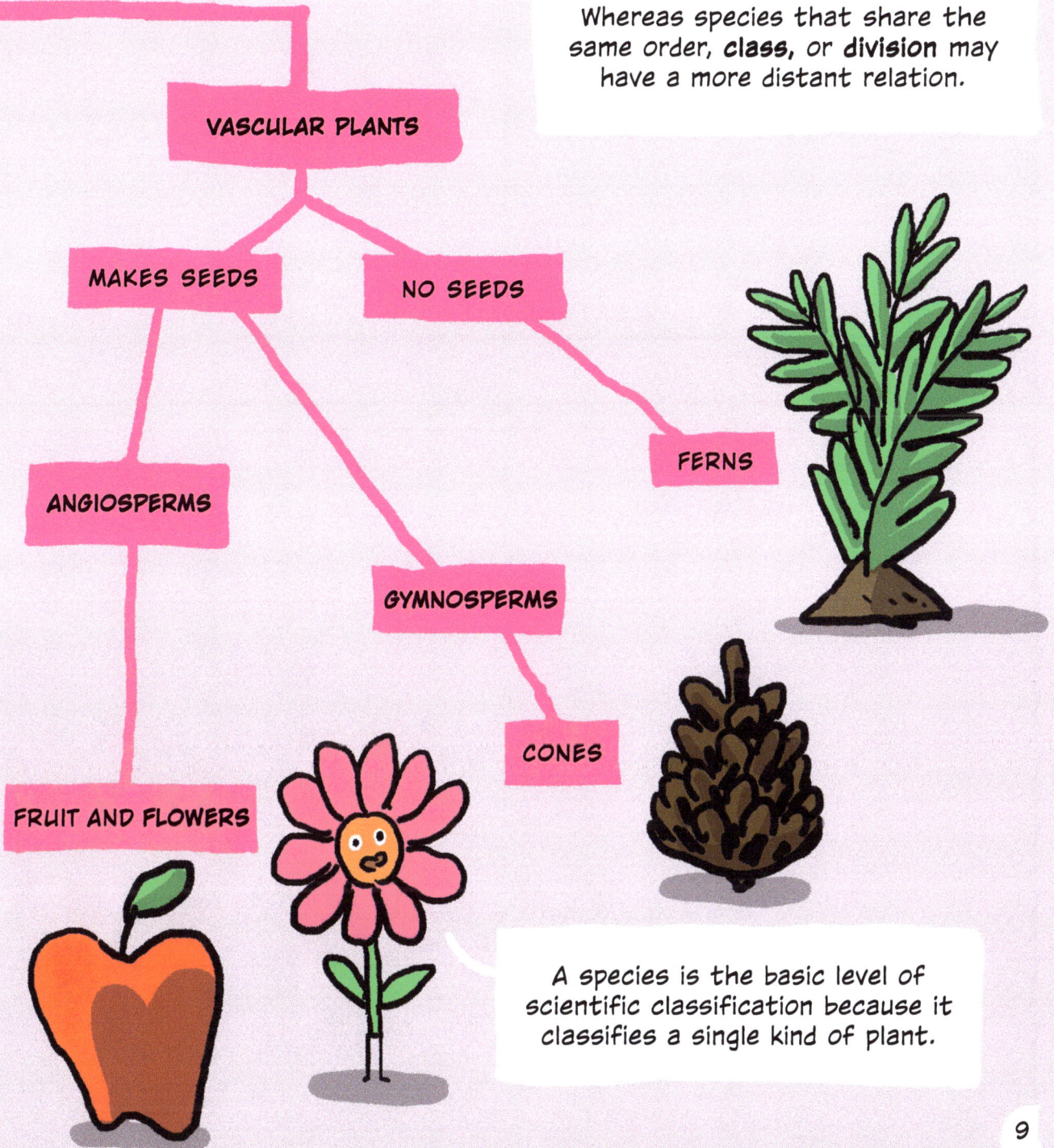

VASCULAR PLANTS

MAKES SEEDS

NO SEEDS

ANGIOSPERMS

FERNS

GYMNOSPERMS

FRUIT AND FLOWERS

CONES

A species is the basic level of scientific classification because it classifies a single kind of plant.

THE PLANT KINGDOM

There are many kingdoms within the scientific classification, including animals, plants, tiny microbes called bacteria, protists, and fungi.

Like the animal kingdom, the members of the plant kingdom can vary in dramatic ways.

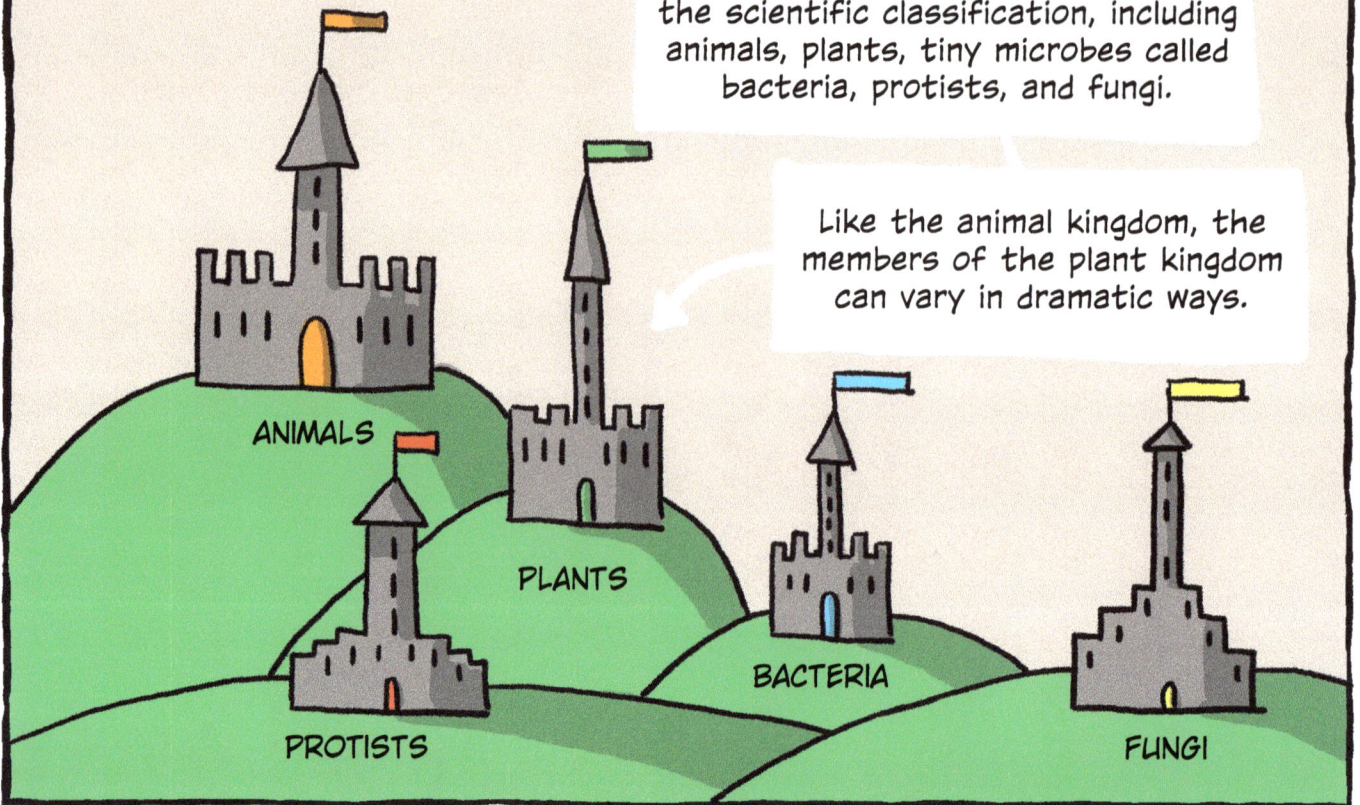

ANIMALS

PLANTS

PROTISTS

BACTERIA

FUNGI

Some tiny plants that grow on the forest floor can barely be seen.

At the same time, sequoia trees rank among the largest living things on Earth.

Some stand over 250 feet (76 meters) tall and have trunks over 30 feet (9 meters) in diameter.

Some plants have extremely long **life spans.**

A bristlecone pine tree in California, for example, has been growing for over 4,600 years.

Other plants live only a few days.

Huh?!

The common duckweed plant is the smallest flowering plant known and lives for only about 30 days.

No matter how different two plants might be, they are more closely related to each other...

...than to any animals, bacteria, fungi, or protists.

Hi!

Hello.

CLASSES OF PLANTS

Within the plant kingdom, plants are classified into large groups and a number of divisions.

One major group consists of **vascular plants.**

Vascular plants contain specialized tissues that carry water and food from one part of the plant to another.

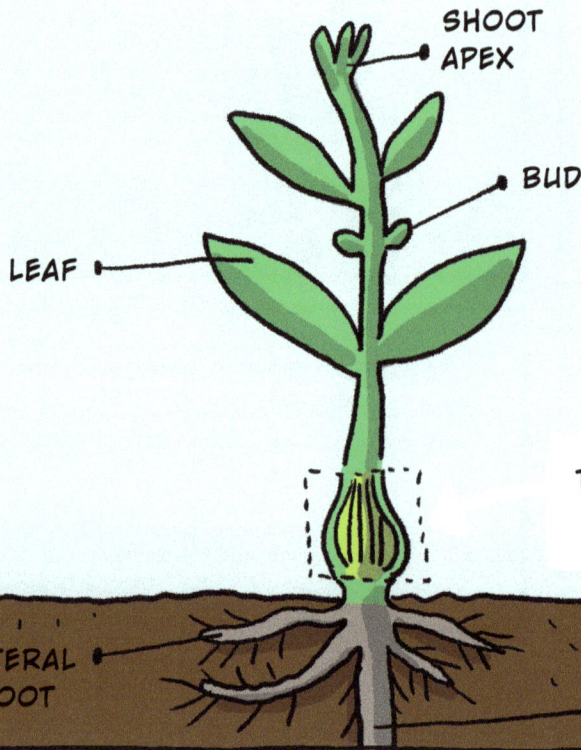

SHOOT APEX

BUD

LEAF

These tissues are called vascular tissue.

The majority of all plants have vascular tissue.

LATERAL ROOT

PRIMARY ROOT

Another major group of plants contains **nonvascular plants.**

These types of plants lack vascular tissue.

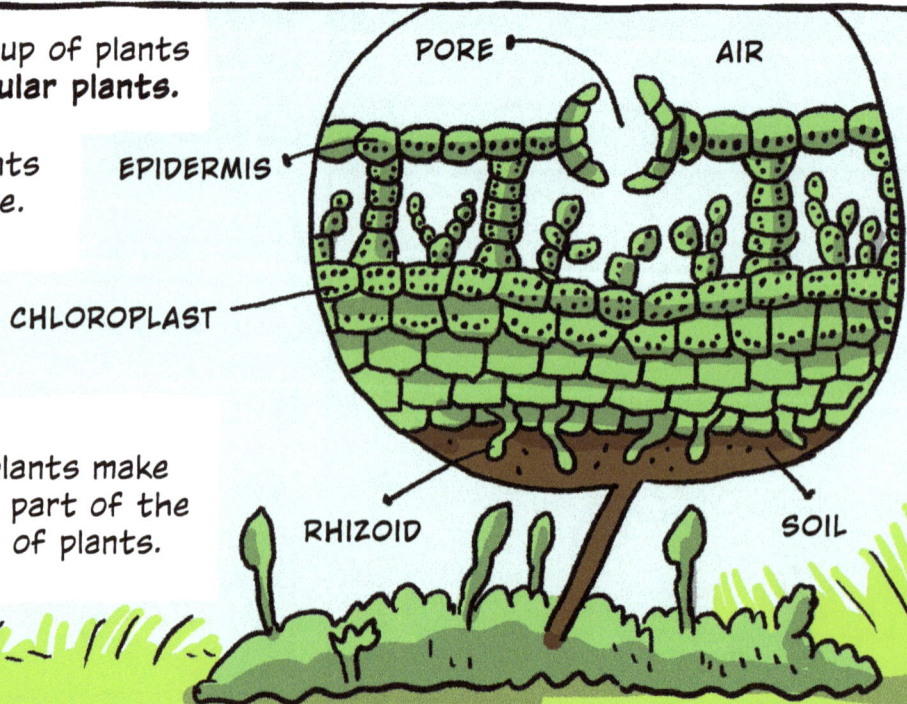

PORE

AIR

EPIDERMIS

CHLOROPLAST

Nonvascular plants make up only a small part of the total number of plants.

RHIZOID

SOIL

Nonvascular plants typically grow in moist, shady places such as forests and ravines.

Most hornworts, liverworts, and mosses measure less than 8 inches (20 centimeters) tall.

MOSS

HORNWORT

LIVERWORT

None of these nonvascular plants have true roots.

Instead, hairy, rootlike growths anchor them to the soil and absorb water and minerals.

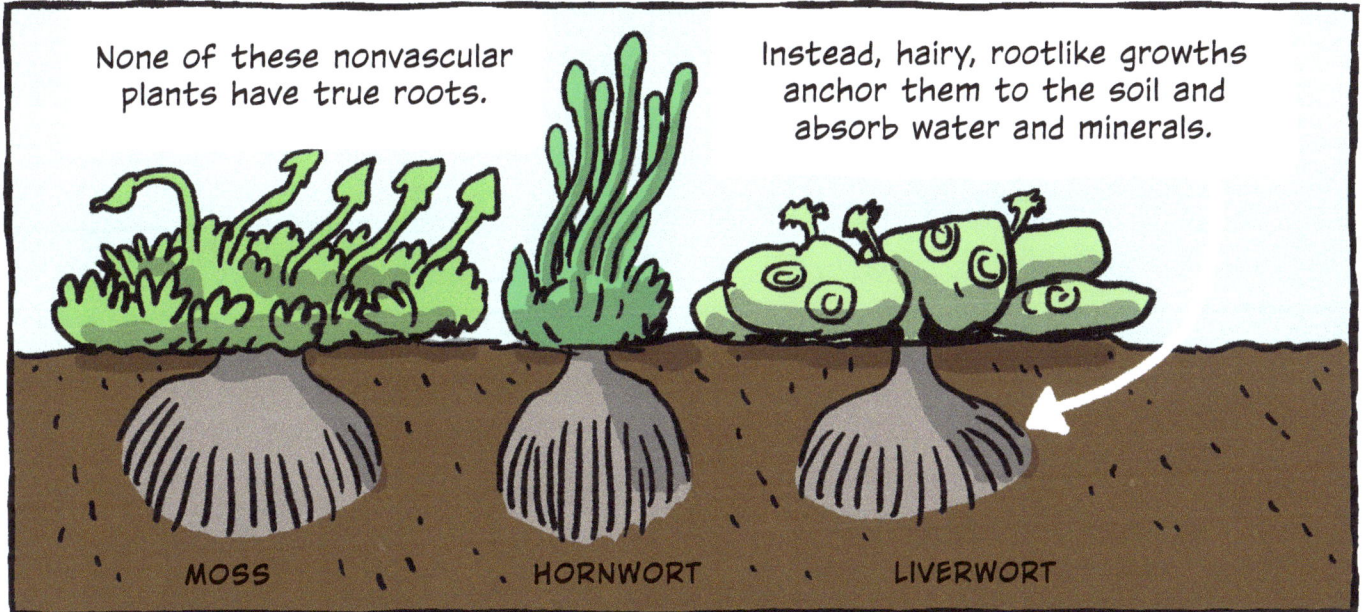

MOSS

HORNWORT

LIVERWORT

Within the vascular group are several smaller groupings, including divisions, classes, orders, families, and more!

WHAT'S IN A NAME?

Pinus resinosa is the **scientific name** of the red pine.

One reason Latin and Greek words are used in scientific classification is that they are not usually used in everyday conversation.

A scientific name is made up of the genus and species of an organism.

Scientific names are useful because common names can be confusing.

For example, you might call this Japanese black pine, "a pine," "tree," or "conifer."

You'd be right!

ROOTS AND STEMS

Vascular plants share many of the same basic **structures,** or parts.

The **roots** of most plants grow underground and help hold the plant in one place.

Unless someone or something moves them, plants stay rooted for their entire lives.

POP

Roots take in water and nutrients from the soil that the plant needs to grow.

Some roots store food for plants.

You've probably eaten the roots of some plants!

Carrots, beets, and radishes are all plant roots.

garden

Most plants have a support structure called a **stem**.

The stem makes up the largest parts of some plants.

The trunk, branches, and twigs of trees are all stems.

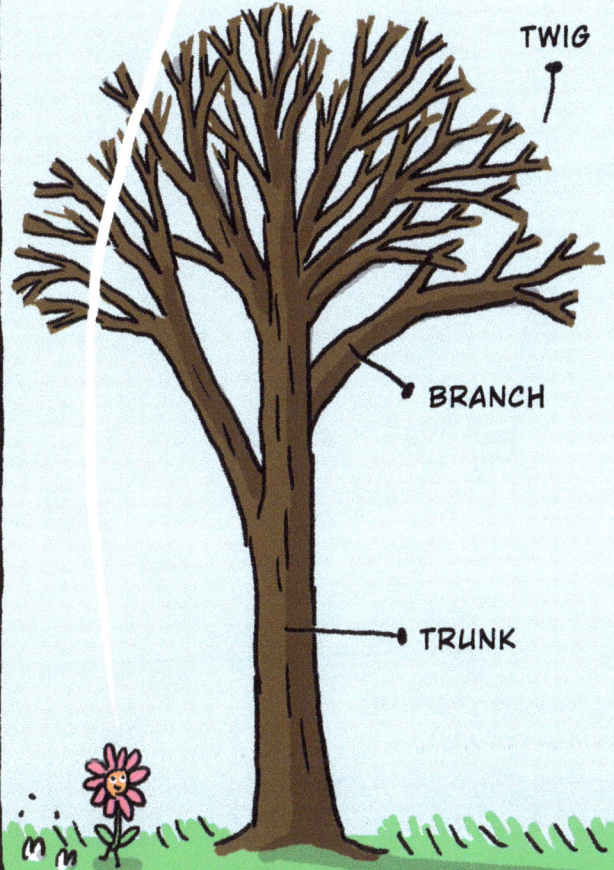

TWIG

BRANCH

TRUNK

Most plants have stems that grow upright and support the other parts of the plant.

By holding the plant up in the air, stems can help a plant receive sunlight.

LEAVES

Plants make their own energy by using sunlight, gases in the air, and water.

This process, specific to plants, is called **photosynthesis.**

Most plants have another special structure called a **leaf.**

Leaves come in many shapes and sizes, but they all play an important part in photosynthesis.

SUNLIGHT PROVIDES ENERGY

OXYGEN IS RELEASED

CARBON DIOXIDE IS TAKEN IN

WATER

You can tell some plants apart by the shape and structure of their leaves.

Rake Rake

Many plants, like oak trees and sunflowers, have wide, flat leaves.

CANNONBALL!

POOF

The edges may be smooth...

...or wavy...

...or ridged.

Grass plants have long, slender leaves.

Pine trees have needle-shaped leaves, and cactuses have leaves that are sharp spines.

Plants can be divided further into divisions and classes based on whether they make **seeds** or not.

Thousands of types of plants produce seeds.

Only a few vascular plants, such as ferns, do not make seeds.

Seed plants can be divided again into orders and families, and eventually classified as a single species of plant.

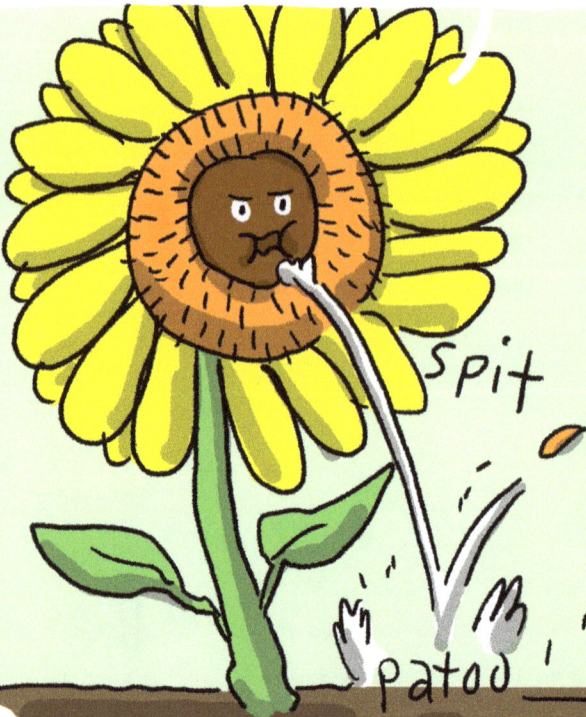

spit

patoo

Some seed plants produce **flowers** and fruits.

These types of plants are classified as **angiosperms.**

The smallest flowering plants, the duckweeds, are only about 1/16 inch (1.6 millimeter) long.

That's tiny!

20

The largest angiosperms are eucalyptus trees.

They grow over 300 feet (90 meters) tall.

In the right environment, a seed can grow into an entirely new plant.

munch munch

FLOWERS AND FRUITS

Most seed plants produce special reproductive structures, such as flowers.

Seeds are manufactured inside these complex and colorful structures.

Some seed plants, such as pine trees, do not produce flowers.

These types of plants are classified as **gymnosperms.**

Pine trees make pine cones instead.

Flowering oak trees make fruits called acorns.

The flowers of most angiosperms start out as buds.

The petals are the largest, most colorful part of most flowers.

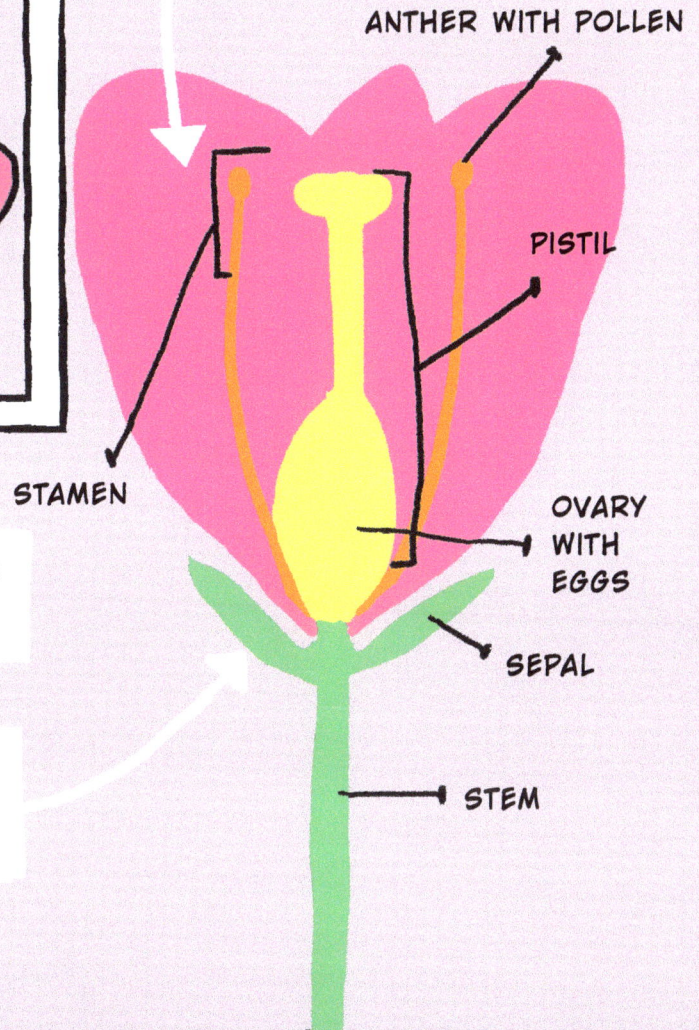

ANTHER WITH POLLEN

PISTIL

STAMEN

OVARY WITH EGGS

At the top of the stem, there are small, leafy parts called sepals.

SEPAL

The sepals protect the bud before the flower blossoms.

STEM

By looking at and comparing the number, shape, arrangement, and color of the flower petals...

...scientists can classify plants into genus and, finally, species!

Let's use this botany guide book to help us classify this plant further.

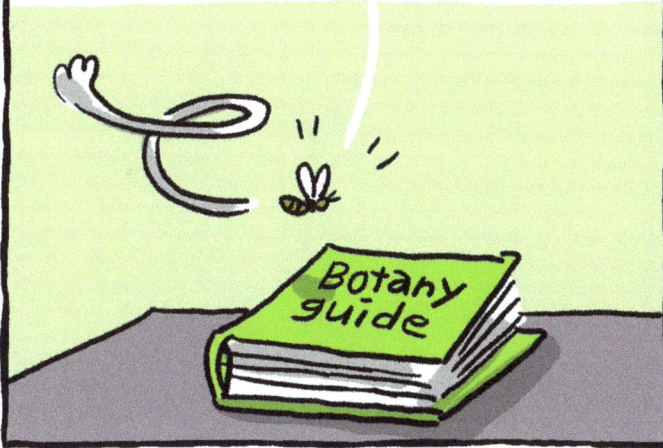

BBBBZ

Hmm. Order is Gentianales...

plop

Family is Rubiaceae...

Genus is Gardenia...

Ah, yes!

I would say it is *Gardenia brighamii*.

BZZ

A forest gardenia!

HELPING PLANTS

Imagine a world without plants...

...there would be no breathable air, no food, and you would not be reading this book!

Houses, furniture, tools, and many other useful products are made out of lumber from trees.

POOF

HEY!

The fibers of bamboo, cotton, and flax plants supply materials to make clothing.

This isn't funny!

But you don't just need plants. They need you too!

POOF

They do?!

Many plants have enlisted animals to help them grow and reproduce.

Insects are drawn to flowers because they can see amazing patterns on the petals that other animals might not see right away.

When an insect is attracted to a flower for food, it can carry **pollen** from one plant to the next.

Off to the next one!

YUMMY!

Plants have developed many different methods to attract animals...

...all in the name of survival!

THE IMPORTANCE OF PLANTS

As more and more humans live on the planet...

...food, its production, and its availability have become a big worry.

Learning how to classify plants and their structures is more important than ever before.

By understanding the taxonomy of plants, you can tell if a plant is helpful to you—

—or poisonous!

scratch scratch

Knowing the difference between a vascular...

...and a nonvascular plant can tell you how to care for a plant and what to expect from it.

Some people remember the levels of plant classification with a special sentence, like this one:

Koalas Drink Cocoa On Foggy Gloomy Sundays.

glug glug glug

The starting letter of each word is also the starting letter of each level of classification:

Kingdom, Division, Class, Order, Family, Genus, and Species.

Try to come up with your own!

K D C O F G S

Now, anytime you recognize a plant, you can try your hand at classification!

GLOSSARY

angiosperm a flowering plant.

botany; botanist the study of plants; a scientist who studies plants.

class a group of living things that share more characteristics than do other members of a phylum.

common descent a way to classify plants by dividing them into smaller groups that share an ancestor.

division a large group of many different kinds of living things that are more alike than those in a kingdom.

domain the highest level of scientific classification that holds the widest grouping of living things.

family a group of living things that are even more alike than those in an order.

flower part of some plants that produces seeds.

genus; genera a smaller group of living things that are very similar but can not mate with one another; more than one genus.

gymnosperm a nonflowering plant.

kingdom the second highest level of scientific classification that holds a wide grouping of living things, such as all animals or all plants.

leaf part of a plant that produces food for the plant.

life span the measure of how long an organism can live in the wild.

nonvascular plant a plant that lacks vascular tissue.

order a group of living things that are more alike than those in a class.

organism any living thing.

photosynthesis the process by which plants make their own food.

plant kingdom (Plantae) a kingdom made up of living things that make their own food using the energy in sunlight.

pollen a fine, yellowish powder formed in a flower that fertilizes a plant's egg.

root part of a plant that collects water and nutrients.

scientific classification a leveled system by which scientists arrange living things into groups.

scientific name a special two-word name, created by combining the genus and species names, used to identify each individual organism.

seed the structure from which plants grow.

species the lowest level of scientific classification, made up of closely related living things with many similarities.

stem the stalk that supports the body of a plant.

structure a body part of a living thing.

taxonomy the science of naming and classifying living things.

trait a physical or behavioral characteristic.

vascular plant a plant that has tissues that carry water and food throughout the plant.

FIND OUT MORE

Books

Backyard Biology: Investigate Habitats Outside Your Door with 25 Projects
by Donna Latham and Beth Hetland
(Nomad Press, 2013)

Plant
by David Burnie
(DK Publishing, 2011)

The Plant Hunters: True Stories of Their Daring Adventures to the Far Corners of the Earth
by Anita Silvey
(Farrar Straus Giroux, 2012)

Plant Parts
by Louise Spilsbury and Richard Spilsbury
(Heinemann, 2008)

Plant Variation and Classification
by Carol Ballard
(Rosen Central, 2010)

Plants: Flowering Plants, Ferns, Mosses, and Other Plants
by Shar Levine and Leslie Johnstone
(Crabtree, 2010)

The Secret Lives of Plants!
by Janet Slingerland and Oksana Kemarskaya
(Capstone, 2012)

Websites

BBC Nature: Plants
http://www.bbc.co.uk/nature/life/Plant
Sample numerous short wildlife videos that identify and discuss unique species of plants on Earth.

Missouri Botanical Garden: Biology of Plant
http://www.mbgnet.net/bioplants/main.html
Make your way through this comprehensive lesson to learn about plant structures, seeds, photosynthesis, and more!

Natural Museum of History: Carl Linnaeus
http://www.nhm.ac.uk/nature-online/science-of-natural-history/biographies/linnaeus/index.html
Meet Carl Linnaeus—the influential scientist who helped develop scientific classification!

National Geographic: Green Plants
http://video.nationalgeographic.com/video/kids/green-kids/plants-kids/
Discover why plants are so important to life on Earth as you watch this brief nature video.

New York Botanical Garden: Plant Hunters
http://www.nybg.org/planthunters/
Become a plant hunter as you explore a virtual conservatory and compete in several plant challenges!

Scholastic Teachers: Science Study Jams!
http://studyjams.scholastic.com/studyjams/jams/science/index.htm
All of your questions about plant and animal life will be answered in clickable lessons featuring narrated slideshows, key terms, and short quizzes.

Science Up Close: Parts of a Flower
http://www.harcourtschool.com/activity/science_up_close/213/deploy/interface.html
Examine a diagram of a plant and click each structure to find out more.

INDEX